# GROUNDING

# AND

# CLEARING

## BEING PRESENT IN THE NEW AGE

## MAYA COINTREAU

# GROUNDING

# AND

# CLEARING

BEING PRESENT IN THE NEW AGE

AN EARTH LODGE® GUIDE

BY MAYA COINTREAU

Earth Lodge

An Earth Lodge® Publication
Gaylordsville, Connecticut

Printed & Published in the U.S.A. by Earth Lodge®
Earth Lodge® is a registered trademark of IPLN, Inc.

ISBN 978-0-6152-10803

*Other books by Maya Cointreau:*


Natural Animal Healing
An Earth Lodge® Guide to Pet Wellness


Equine Herbs & Healing
An Earth Lodge® Guide to Horse Wellness


To The Temples
14 Meditations for Healing & Guidance


Breaking Eight


The Book of Cookbooks, Volume II

This book is dedicated to all the lightworkers, the angels on earth, the leaders and the teachers, and the lost and confused, to all of you who strive to make this world a better place.

You are doing it.

Thank you.

*Therefore I say unto you,*
*Whatever you desire,*
*when you pray,*
*believe that you receive them,*
*and you shall have them.*


Mark 11:24

# TABLE of CONTENTS

# Why I Wrote This Book

## Or

## Our Need to Ground and Clear

I decided to write this book in November of 2006, while placing an order for books at my holistic healing center in Connecticut. We were looking for new books to expand our reference section, and needed some good tomes on grounding. We already had books on healing, on herbs, on auras and chakras. Books on past lives and out of body experiences. What our clients were asking for more help with was grounding. So imagine my surprise when I could not find one title to purchase. Not one book on such a basic topic.

Suddenly everything slid into focus. It is no coincidence that the general public views metaphysical topics as "flighty," "spacey" and "insubstantial." In the New Age, we spend much of our time and energy looking for new ways to open the third eye, to heighten our awareness, to vibrate and ascend to new and higher levels. Countless books and classes teach these topics and more, and grounding, when mentioned, is an afterthought.

## WE CAN ONLY BIRTH A NEW REALITY IF WE ARE GROUNDED IN THE PHYSICAL.

Our souls have attached to our physical bodies for just this purpose. In order to receive, embody and enact the messages that our higher selves send us, our bodies must be strong and aligned right along with our chakras.

We can not hear the messages we were meant to hear when we are not grounded. Without grounding, any energy we raise may be misdirected and uncontained.

Feeling confused? Too many dreams, too many messages?

This book is meant to give you the tools you need to remain a focused and clear channel for your higher self. With regular grounding and clearing, you can remain calm and assured while you free your spiritual gifts. A clear channel without distortion, miracles and messages will manifest everyday.

There is no mystery to the grounding techniques detailed in this book – with good intent, even small efforts at grounding will yield potent results.

# INTENT

Intention. Will. Clear, focused intent will always lead to the proper outcome in the end. Intent is everything. Lately I have found that sometimes just by intending to do a healing or similar spiritual work, it is already done before I begin. Other lightworkers have spoken of similar "miracles" occurring in their work. These healers all have one thing in common – they are all grounded, and their will is clear. When they work, they are calm. They are assured. They are clear channels with no distortions.

We can raise all the energy we want for spiritual work, but it is through grounding that we manifest our psychic creations into this reality.

## Collecting Light

There is an old shamanic method of collecting energy and calming the mind that works very well to focus the will. This exercise works best with the sun, but anything that gives off light will work: candles, fireplaces, light bulbs, the moon. I do not recommend using fluorescent light sources for this exercise (or indeed anytime you need to be focused) as studies have shown that they interfere significantly with memory and concentration.

Sit comfortably and relax. Close your eyes most of the way, so you are looking through your eyelashes. Let your lashes catch the light of the sun or candle, without looking directly at it, and slowly turn your head from side to side, drinking the light through your eyes deep into your soul. Feel the light flow through you, feeding you, relaxing you and bring you to your higher purpose. Do this for ten to twenty minutes, until you feel sated.

## Working with Intention

Once you feel ready to get to work, whatever your work may be, you must begin with clear intentions. Whatever you intend, you will achieve. If you want to do something, but do not believe in it with every fiber of your being, you will not have an easy time achieving it. But if you believe, if you have faith, *if you have a very clear idea of exactly what is you want to achieve and you have every expectation that you will achieve it*, there will be no stopping you.

The key is *intent. Intent* is more than just sort of, kind of, wanting to do something. Intent is about really wanting it. Really *meaning* it. Intent is about clarity of purpose, single-mindedness of will. As Yoda so aptly put it in *Star Wars*: "Do, or do not. There is no try."

Never set out to "try" something. It most likely will not get finished, and it will not be pleasant, either: related to the punitive words trial, or test, as it is. Set out to *do* everything, and things will get done.

The key to this process of doing is to be very, very clear about what it is you would like to get done. The clearer your mind is about what you expect, the easier and more in line with your expectations the results will be.

Personally, I like to do a painting or make a list of what I expect to achieve, or rather what I *have achieved,* for once I conceive of it is already created, I have but to receive it. This a belief I have picked up from studies of quantum physics, where particles in experiments behave how one *expects* them to behave. Once the scientist conceives of a new particle he would like to find, he finds it; once he imagines new and strange behavior he'd like to see – boom! – there it is, zipping through its paces in the particle accelerator.

If all single particles behave this way, then surely all matter behaves this way, and thus, all physical reality.

That which you expect, manifests. That which you believe, is.

# How to Use the Guide

There are infinite methods available to us for grounding and clearing. This book organizes many of these methods into categories. First, read through the book. Later, you can use the book for reference, but it will be easier to do so in a pinch if you are already familiar with all the chapters. You will most likely find that some chapters and methods resonate strongly with you, while others may not interest you at all. Great! You may even decide that you like the ideas in this guide, but that you are only going to use them as a springboard to create your own grounding or clearing routines – even better!

The important thing is that you begin to do the work of grounding and clearing on a regular basis. Every being, and every space, needs this work on Planet Earth. We all affect each other, and so we all need to be cleared from time to time. This guide is just another tool to help you find your way through life in an uplifting, empowered manner.

## Choosing a Method

Not sure which method to choose for a particular situation? Generally, I recommend following your gut, your intuition, as those inner feelings are actually our greater self's way of trying to get in touch with us to let us know what will most benefit us. Still, sometimes it's nice to get a little extra confirmation.

One way you can choose which method to work with is by dowsing with a pendulum. Pendulums are basic tools used by dowsers for centuries to find water and ley lines (energy meridians on the earth's surface.) You can find pendulums in most new age shops, usually consisting of a nice, heavy stone on one end of a short chain, with a smaller stone or ring on the other end. You can also use a pointed pendant or cross on a necklace chain as a pendulum.

To use a pendulum, hold the smaller end by one hand so that the large stone or pendant hangs a few inches over your other hand, palm up and open. In your mind, intend that only your greater self or your guides of the light can communicate through the tool. Ask it to show you how it swings for "Yes." This may be vertical, horizontal, clockwise, or counter-clockwise. Then, ask it to show you "No." Confirm your results by asking it a yes or no questions to which you know the answer, such as "Is my birthday in December?"

To choose a method by dowsing, you can then open the book to the table of contents, and ask if the best method is in the chapter on stones? No. Ok, how about the next chapter? And so on, until you find you answer. You may want to go through every chapter, in case your guides want you to use several methods together.

Another way to receive yes or no answers is through kinesiology. Kinesiology, or muscle-testing, works with your body to see what will work best for you. In Kinesiology, that which makes your muscles stronger is good, and that which makes you weak should be avoided. You can muscle test yourself by making a circle on one hand with your thumb and index finger. Then, insert the thumb and index finger from the other hand together into the circle up to the first joint, and open them, trying to split the circle of your other hand, while you try to hold it shut. Normally, you should be able to keep the circle intact without difficulty. Now, think of a food that disagrees with you and ask, "Do I like this food?" If kinesiology is working for you, the circle should burst open, essentially saying "No!"

You can also muscle-test other people, which is often more fool-proof because our ego can not get in the way. To muscle test another person, have them hold one arm out straight to the side, and tell them to try and hold it in this position while you gently but firmly push down above their wrist. Take note of how far you were able to dip their arm (usually only a few inches) and then in your head think of what you are testing for (for foods, vitamins, colors, etc, you can also have them not look while you put an item in their other hand to be tested.) If their arm dips the same as before, that is a "Yes" but if it dips far lower you have a "No." Muscle-testing takes practice to get the hang of, but once you've got it, you can never be caught without it.

Another fun method of choosing a way to ground or clear with this book is to sit with your eyes closed, clear your mind, and then begin to slowly flip the pages of the book from one end to the other. When you feel you're on the right page, stop. Look at where you are, and give that section's advice a go.

As we discussed in the previous chapter, there is no right or wrong way to use this book. Have fun with it. Experiment. You do not need to master every technique in this book to become grounded. You do not need to clear yourself every moment of the day to be free from external influences. Practice, and you will see how different situations, people and places affect you. Only then will *you* be able to determine what you need to do.

# GROUNDING & CLEARING

# WITH STONES

Stones, used properly, are an obvious and powerful choice for grounding. Of the earth, they are good channels for free-floating energy. The key is to pick the right stone for your purpose. A meteorite, such as moldavite, may be beautiful and intriguing, but it is not going to bring you back down to earth. Pyramid shaped stones, like naturally-occurring apophyllite or carved pyramids, raise energy and open the crown chakra to the heavens, but do nothing to connect that heavenly energy to the body's lower extremities and down through the earth.

Most stones used for healing and chosen by the new age community in general are not grounding. They do wondrous and beautiful miracles. They connect us with the higher planes. They bring love and healing into our lives. Many of them do clear the chakras and the body, but few are adept at helping to ground us. By using only stones that open us, and not combining them with grounding, protective stones, we are left open to mixed messages and misdirected energy.

I recommend that everyone who works with stones always have a few good grounding stones on hand, and this chapter gives you many wonderful choices. The stones listed here provide consistent earth energy, steady and clarifying. They are not always the most exciting or sparkling gems in the case, but they will remain faithfully yours: virile, protective and strong allies as you climb the ladder of ascension.

### Agate

All agates are gently grounding, and soothe and calm the nerves. They help build confidence and self-reliance. Agate comes in almost every color, each of which corresponds to different chakras to further help with chakra specific issues. For example, green agate helps heal the heart and lungs, while helping to ground one through live plant energy. Yellow agate helps connect one to the divine and clears stomach issues, while also clearing the aura with sun energy. Agates are particularly well-suited for children and pets, due to their gentle, nurturing disposition.

## Black Tourmaline

Tourmaline allows you to get to the root of problems and negativity. Black tourmaline in particular is a grounding stone with very high vibrations, and shields the wearer from negativity of all kinds, including electromagnetic waves and radiation. My favorite tourmaline specimens for grounding consist of the black rods at least the size of one's pinkie finger growing through clear or white quartz – they have a wonderfully clean effect on illnesses and the environment. It draws earth energy through the root chakra to increase one's vitality and energy.

## Bloodstone

Far and away my favorite grounding stone, this dark green quartz stone is said to have received its red iron flecks from the blood of Christ at the crucifixion and is traditionally believed to be capable of miracle healings. Bloodstone is indeed a powerful healer, cleansing the blood, liver and reproductive systems, and is helpful in all dis-eases. It activates the root and heart chakras and draws energy from the earth directly through the legs and reproductive organs, dispersing energy equally throughout the entire body via the circulatory system and the meridians. It is a comforting, protective stone that brings calm and reassurance to the wearer, lowering the heart rate and blood pressure while soothing the soul.

## Boji Stones/ Kansas Pop Rocks

Boji stones come from the base of a natural pyramid-shaped hill in at the heart of the United States in Kansas, and help to center and balance the individual. They can be bought and used in pairs, one female and one male, to balance yin and yang energy. The female stones generally have smooth surfaces, and the males rough. They direct excess energy into the earth and help keep the holder rooted on earth, in the physical. Boji stones can be used with great success to bring people "back to earth" when they get too flighty or spacey, and help counteract excess or disruptive geopathic and environmental energies.

## Calcite

Calcite is a gentle, friendly stone that helps clear disturbances in energy fields be they geopathic, electromagnetic, or in the body. Use calcite to clear your energy when you feel you are picking up to much energy from people around you, or when you are over-stimulated. Calcite comes in many colors and opacities, but the clear or translucent varieties are best for this purpose.

## Carnelian

Carnelian energizes the physical body and stimulates healthful activity while grounding. Excess energy from the upper chakras is transmuted by carnelian into physical strength and vitality. This beautiful reddish to brown stone helps facilitate a constant exchange of this energy with the earth, allowing the wearer to become one with her surroundings. Negativity rolls off the back when one bears this stone, making the bearer impervious to ill will from others. It helps heal wounds of the heart and body.

## Chlorite

Chlorite is a beautiful green stone, often found in combinations with clear quartz crystals. It has a reputation for clearing toxins and negativity from the body. It can be used to clear miasms, underlying genetic and karmic diseases, from the body.

## Danburite

Whether we spend too much time in our upper chakras and out of our bodies, or our souls are still not sure that incarnating was the best idea, danburite helps us feel more comfortable in our bodies and brings us back to reality while facilitating an open channel to our higher selves. The pink pieces have a particularly soothing effect, though all danburite is calming. For these purposes I recommend the clear, brown or pink hues rather than the lilac.

## Garnet

Deep, dark red garnet is very similar to bloodstone in its properties, with its healing effect more focused on the blood and sexual organs rather than the entire body. It has the further effect of enhancing sexuality and virility, and is one of the best stones to awaken and open the root chakra.

### Granite

Heat and shock resistant, granite is happy to lend us its strength and help us connect with the earth. Food prepared on granite countertops often tastes fresher, and it has the power to help transmute pesticides used on non-organic crops. Place your hands on the countertop and take a few deep breaths, letting your frustrations of the day be cleared and the good strong energy of the granite infuse you.

### Hematite

Hematite is a very yang, or male, stone of a dark silver color. It works very well with men to protect them from negativity and balance their testosterone. Reflective yet magnetic, hematite will draw negativity and illness off of the bearer and reflect it back to whence it came. For this reason it needs regular weekly or even daily cleansing depending on the intensity of its use. To cleanse Hematite, place it in a bowl of cold water in a window overnight.

## Kyanite

This wonderful stone clears and aligns the chakras of all those who come near it. When it is worn, it has a constant protective and grounding effect as it clears and aligns, clears and aligns, over and over again. The bearer of this stone is quite difficult to knock off-balance energetically. Because the chakras are aligned and open, one's higher self and energy body are able to enter the physical body, leading to higher ascension and attunements. Kyanite is easily found in many shades of blue and blue-green, as well as black: black Kyanite is more protective but less aligning than blue Kyanite.

## Leopardskin Jasper

This particular jasper allows one to get in touch with animals and the forest/jungle aspect of the earth. It facilitates animal communication and shapeshifting, which is essentially the transmutation of one's higher purpose within the physical. It allows the manifestation of one's will on the earthly plane. It calls in the protection of the large cats to the wearer, and allows one to become one with one's surroundings and the earth, making it easier to ground.

## Obsidian/Apache Tears

Obsidian is one of the most grounding, protective stones you can find. Obsidian looks opaque, but is actually translucent, which helps allow us to see through the negativity to the positive, and vice versa, to see what is hidden. Apache Tears are a particular variety of obsidian that is steeped in legend, and has the added quality of helping one cope with issues of anger, grief, and forgiveness. Apache storytellers say that one day a group of Apaches was ambushed by an enemy tribe (recent versions have transmuted the tribe into a white man's cavalry) and in the fight they were cornered and forced over a cliff to their deaths. When the women found them, they wept long and hard, and as their tears struck the ground, each tear was transformed into small, round pieces of obsidian. When you carry an Apache Tear, legend says, you will never cry, for the women shed enough tears for all.

## Onyx

Onyx can be found in many earthy colors, including brown, green, and black. Long used as a popular stone for men's jewelry, onyx has a warm, safe, feeling. The green can be mossy or brilliant, and is good for healing and connecting to nature. Brown onyx helps kundalini energy flow up and through the root chakra, and remediates many reproductive issues. Black onyx is good or shielding one from negativity and lending the wearer courage and strength.

## Petrified Wood

Petrified wood is not a stone, per se, but ancient wood which has fossilized over the millennia to form a light, stone like substance. Jet is a form of black, petrified wood that has been used in jewelry for centuries. All petrified wood helps root us to the earth while filtering out toxic thoughts and patterns from our DNA, much as live plants filter and purify the air and water, which passes through them.

## Prehnite

This light minty green to blue stone can often be found among gray gravel driveways, roads and ditches. It is considered very protective, while also stimulating energy flow throughout the body and encouraging enhanced spiritual communication, meditation and astral travel.

## Rainbow Fluorite

Fluorite with green and purple is called rainbow fluorite. The purple color connects the third eye and crown chakras with the body and heart, the green color. It is a fantastic stone for clearing and balancing excess energy, while facilitating psychic opening and growth. It is a healing stone for the heart and the mind. It regulates the flow of energy into the upper body and allows it to pass through the torso to the legs, making it easier to ground. It works very well with *selenite* to clear negativity from the environment, and worn with black tourmaline will allow the kundalini to flow easily through the entire body. Place a large piece in the center of a room or each corner of a house to eliminate geopathic stress.

## Ruby

Ruby opens and awakens the root and heart chakras, returning them to full vitality. It allows the fully feminine and creative earth energy of Gaia to enter the body, making one feel vibrant, whole, and in touch with their sexuality. If there is anger blocking the progress of one's relationships, it will be brought out into the open and blasted away with the power of Kali, the devourer goddess. On the physical level, ruby restores balance to the reproductive system and attending hormones.

### Selenite

Passed through the aura and around the body, selenite will cut cords and remove energy drains. Placed in a room it will clear geopathic and electromagnetic stress, as well as any other form of negativity. It is so good at clearing that the stone itself never needs to be cleansed, as it will never hold negative energy itself. *Note: Do not wash or immerse selenite, it is water-soluble and may dissolve.*

### Shaman Stones/Moqui Balls

Shaman stones, or moqui balls, are found in the Moqui Desert. Balls of sandstone coated with iron ore, they are believed to have formed when a giant meteor struck the earth and flash-melted the iron present in the sand. They are prized for their ability to help facilitate meditative states and trance journeys while still keeping one linked to their physical body. Both alien and terrestrial, shaman stones offer an unusual link between realities and dimensions. They offer an anchor to those who would travel between different planes of realities, so that one can easily return to one's body and time. Once through with trance work, shaman stones are also ideal for re-grounding and clearing one's head.


## Shiva Lingham Stones

Shiva Lingham stones are oblong stones from the holy Narmada River in India, naturally formed into an egg-like shape by eons of water flow, and then further smoothed by the hands of man. In India it is believed that these stones are direct links to Shiva and the fiery pillar of creation, and when you hold these stones in your hands, you are holding the power of the god Shiva in your hands. Considered holy in India (remember India Jones & The Temple of Doom? That was a radiant Shiva Lingham stone the village lost.) they can be used to activate the root chakra and heal sexual and reproductive organs. They are believed to unify feminine and masculine energy into creative harmony. A Shiva Lingham placed in a bedroom encourages passion; held in meditation, it creates a strong connection with both the creative energies of the feminine and with male potency. It is a powerful stone for willful manifestation.

## Slate

Slate is an old, old stone and soul, and brings us the wisdom of the ages. Its many layers allow us to read between the lines and find understanding on all levels. It contains the peace of the elderly, the knowledge that time has no bounds, and can bring that same peace and serenity to those who would work with it. A path of slate to your front door will wipe away the mundane cares and worries of all who tread it.

## Smoky Quartz

Smoky Quartz is a dependable grounding stone that shields one from psychic harm when placed in the room. In its natural state, smoky quartz also carries the clearing properties that open the crown chakra, allowing the dual energies of the earth and the higher realms to flow freely in and out of the body through both the crown and root chakras. In its irradiated state smoky quartz works only with root chakra, while its protective qualities take on an almost fierce nature, become extremely loyal and guarding. I recommend that only smoky quartz in its natural state be chosen for wear, while either state is acceptable for use in one's environment. Tibetan Smoky Quartz has the added benefit of carrying centuries of Buddhist prayer energy within it, helping to facilitate calm serenity in the face of adversity.

## Snowflake Obsidian

Snowflake Obsidian is a sweet, friendly stone for protection and grounding. It will benefit almost anyone. Black with white "snowflake" marks, it seeks to balance yin and yang energy. It works with forgiveness to release anger and allows one to see both sides of things. It connects to both the lower and higher realms, without prejudice. Don't be fooled: despite its easy nature, snowflake obsidian contains great strength and is very, very shielding from negativity. This coupled with its gentle balancing nature make it a wonderful stone for young children to carry with them to school and play dates.

## Soo Chow Marble

Soo Chow Marble from China contains a particularly calm, immovable spirit, more so than that of other marbles which are more likely to harbor the same high energy and sensitivities as the artists who often work with it. Soo Chow, on the other hand, immediately places one deep in the earth, her inner frequencies. This is the stone of the stoic dwarves of the path, the stone that moves time to keep pace with molasses. When you feel hurried or rushed, reach for Soo Chow. Feel your bonds to time release, for you are one with all.

## Tiger's Eye

Tiger's Eye is a beautiful, striped stone of golds, browns, blacks and blues. Sometimes it takes the appearance of a hawk's eye, in which case it is believed to increase insight and understanding in the owner, while the golden examples are used in homes and businesses to increase prosperity and abundance. All tiger's eye is very protective against psychic attacks and ill will, and helps protect travelers. Few are foolish enough to mess with a tiger, and the big cat energy that is held in this stone will hold vigil over those who carry or wear it.

# Grounding & Clearing

# With Nature

There is no better place to ground than on the ground. Mother Nature, Mother Earth, they both want to nurture us, heal us, feed us. The Earth is happiest when her charges are also happy. She can only ascend and raise her vibration when we also ascend and rise in vibration. When we war, she feels our pain. When we cry, she cries. The Earth emits powerful waves of energy from deep within which can be measured with scientific equipment. When our brain waves match her waves, science has shown that our minds are quiet, calm and ready for action.

There are various ways to align with the energy of the Earth and nature to ground and clear our bodies and souls. The first is rather obvious. Get down on the ground!

## On the Ground

Lie or sit on the ground, bare grass, desert sand, on or against a rock, against a tree. Close your eyes and breathe slow, deep breaths.

Feel your body become one with ground, with its surroundings. Imagine that there are roots growing out of your feet, the base of your spine, your hands, growing long and deep, deep in to the earth. Your roots pull up cool, clear water. They feed on the nutrients of the dirt, on the loving energy of the Earth. You are accepted here. There are no feelings of intrusion as your roots grow through the soil, only love, giving and gratitude.

Feel tender leaves budding out of the top of your head, open and receptive to the glow of the sun, the freshness of the air, the cool breathe of the moon. Feelings of refreshment energize you, circulating through your entire body, just as the life-giving sap which rises from your roots circulates, and the two energies mingle together, feeding your soul. You are ageless, enduring, whole. Complete.

## Being with Nature

Of course, sometimes it is not convenient to sit or lie down in nature. It may be raining, cold, or just too difficult to sit still. This is a good time to practice just *being* with nature. All that is required for this is that you are outside: you can be doing yard work, construction outside, walking the dog, or just getting the mail. You do not need to be climbing a mountain (although mountains are wonderful things to climb.)

Take a moment to quiet your mind. Breathe deeply, in and out, in and out. With each breath, with each step, imagine your consciousness expanding up and out, up and out. Ever outward, you consciousness co-mingles with the leaves on the ground and in the trees, the wind that swirls through the air, the birds flying high above. You hear a dog bark in the distance, and you *are* the dog in the distance. Imagine yourself at one with all. Now, with your consciousness expanded and mixed with the nature that surrounds you, practice just *being.*

If a thought enters your head about something mundane, something home- or work-related, just let it go. Just *BE.* Feel the energy of all that surrounds you pass through you, lifting you up. Nature is not worrying about what to buy for dinner. Nature is just *doing, being.*

## Calling the Nature Spirits

Nature spirits, or devas, are the elements, the creative energy of nature, that which keeps nature flowing and in flow. They work and play with the chi of the Earth, and they *are* the chi of the earth. They are many things. They keep the plants growing and the flowers flowering and the wind blowing and sometimes they *are* the wind and the plant and flowers. They work with the rocks and sometimes they *are* the rocks.

There is a hierarchy of nature spirits, and each piece of land has an overlighting deva to whom the fairies answer, who protects you and the land, and helps your plants grow free and strong. "Overlighting" means that they watch over you, while simultaneously bringing more *light* to the area where they are. Together with the angels they watch over the land and the earth. They play with the wind and the trees, the skies and the waters. Devas are more intimately involved in the workings of the nature of the earth than the angels, it is they that the fairies and gnomes patterned themselves after when they decided to become less physical, and more non-physical, and to become more *one* with the energy play of the earth and the devas. Devas have been called nature spirits, sprites and sylphs for many years.

Overlighting angels are a bit more removed. They watch. They help channel energy to the areas they watch. They speak with the devas and feel empathy for all living creatures in their area but they do not intervene on a physical level as much as the fairies or the devas. They will and do help the devas and the humans clear negative energy from areas when they are called in, and they do help connect humanity to Source. But they do not shift the winds or the rains or the sun or make the plants grow swifter or taller. That is the work and the play of the devas and the fairies.

Every piece of earth has an overlighting angel. Some watch small areas of earth, and some watch very large pieces of earth. Most pieces of earth have several overlighting angels watching over them, at different levels, feeling different levels of connection and inter-personal connectedness. So, as your home or street has an overlighting angel, so do your city, and the general area of your state, and the area of your country, and also your entire country. Your entire planet has an overlighting angel called the Sun, and also the Moon.

Devas and angels can be called upon to help re-connect you to the earth or other elements of nature such as the sun, moon, plants or animals. They are particularly attuned to clearing spaces, large or small. Call on overlighting angels to clear geopathic stress, or energetic disturbances in mass consciousness. Devas are great for shutting down black streams of negative energy on your property, negative vortexes or portals to other planes and dimensions. Think about the size of space you want to clean, and then call in the appropriate nature spirit(s). Always ask them respectfully for their help, they do not appreciate being ordered around, but are eager to assist us in any way they can, so long as our motives and our intent are pure.

Be as clear as you can about what you would like them to do, and within minutes, days or weeks, depending on the job you set them to, you will see marked improvements. A simple and heartfelt "Thank You" is always appreciated. Ask if there is anything you can do in return or addition to what they are doing: sometimes you may be asked to put a specific crystal somewhere, or plant a new flower. They may ask you to take a bath in saltwater, or you may hear nothing. All responses are ok. Even if you can not hear the fairies or the angels when they speak to you, trust that they are there, and they *do* hear you! Joyfully, lovingly, for their hearts are pure, they seek to help humanity heal itself and heal the planet around them.

## Working with Flower Essences

Flower essences nourish the soul and harmonize the body by working on an energetic level. Based on homeopathic principles of dilution, flower essences are made with pure water using either vinegar or alcohol as a preservative. The flowers generally sit on or in the water in the sunlight for mere hours, creating mother "tinctures" which carry the energetic imprint of the flower itself. There are a myriad of flower essences on the market today, and many of them are good for clearing various emotional and metaphysical issues, as well as grounding.

*Black-eyed Susan* clears karma and heals anger and guilt. It uplifts the dark, and transmutes it to Light. *Echinacea* and yarrow are wonderful for combating geopathic stress and both are very grounding. *Flowering Raspberry* clears fuzzy thinking and helps return one back to their body.

*Balsam Poplar* is used specifically to ground sexual energy, while *Gladiolus* activates the kundalini and fires the soul, raising the vibration of the body simultaneously. It clears mass consciousness, facilitates transition and enables ascension. *Hollyhock* clears and connects all chakras in all the bodies: etheric, astral, physical, spiritual, mental.

*Fireweed, White Spruce, Rosemary, Calendula* and *Corn* are also all grounding and helpful when trying to connect to the Earth. There are many more wonderful essences out there, look online, at your local health food store, or holistic health center.

## Connecting with the Four Directions

Earth. Air. Fire. Water. North. East. South. West. Each direction has its corresponding element and energy. Together, they represent balance, harmony, and completion. Together, they are strong. When one element is out of balance, the rest are weakened. For grounding and protection, I like to call in the four directions at the beginning of any spiritual work. Together, they surround me with strength and purpose.

The North is the element of Earth and, in some traditions, Metal. It works with the archangel Uriel. The

North is steady, calm and has great depths of understanding and purpose to lend to any cause.

The East is the element of Air, bringing the wisdom of the oracles on its wings. Archangel Raphael is its guardian. It refreshes the soul with the breath of life.

The South is the element of Fire, extremely protective and vigilant. Few will dare to cross it, making the South a fierce, if sometimes unpredictable, ally. It is associated with archangel Michael.

The West is the element of Water, flexible and peaceful. Archangel Gabriel is its representative, and is considered by most to be female. The West is also good for clearing, washing away emotional debris and bringing up what must be seen.

To call in the elements, I like to stand and face each direction, beginning with the North or the East because those are the elements I am most attuned to. Begin with whichever element you feel the most support from. Respectfully call them in, one by one. I raise my arms to the heavens as I lift my head and my voice, and say something along these lines:

"I call to the guardian of the north, ancient element of earth. I ask for you assistance and guidance, please help me now as I seek to ground my energy and clear my home. I thank you for your presence here."

When I feel I am finished, I often go through the process again, thanking each one by saying something like this:

"Guardian of the north, ancient element of earth, I thank you for your presence here. Go in power."

There are many ways to work with the directions. You can honor them by placing things which represent them and their elements about your home, desk or property. A seashell or cup for water, a rock or plant for earth, a feather or wind chime for air, a candle or volcanic rock for fire. There is no one way to go about it. The key, as with everything in this book, is intent. Whatever you intend, you bring about, you create.

For more in-depth work with the elements on a physical level, seek out a certified Polarity Therapist, who works to balance the elements within the body.

# GROUNDING & CLEARING

# WITH BREATH

I have already mentioned the idea of taking deep, slow breaths in this book as a part of several grounding processes. Breathing, on its own, can be a wonderful way to ground. Indeed, it is the true function of breath.

When we breathe, each breath out is an exhalation of toxins, spent energy, old chi. Each inhalation carries fresh air, oxygen to our cells, fuel for our physical bodies and residual energy from plants, stars (including the sun) and basic elements. Each breath is the breath of life. Each breath carries a piece of God, the universal source of life, in it. It is, in its simplicity, All That Is.

When you breathe in, intend to collect all the energy of the universe on that breath. Intend that as the oxygen washes through every cell in your body it is clearing away the old, the tired, the tainted, and leaving only the new, the fresh, the awake. See the energy of the sun and the moon, the stars and the sky, washing through you, enlivening every fiber of your soul and your being.

When you breathe out, intend to release every last tired particle that was cleansed from your cells with that breath. See every old emotion that held you back and tied you to the past bursting out with that breath.

Imagine your exhaled toxins and despairs falling gently to earth, where they become one with the humus, reborn and renewed, becoming new plants, and new air, which you can then breathe in on your next breath.

In. Out.

In.        Out.

In.


Out.

In

and

Out.

Ah.

Another way to ground with breath is to breathe down through your body, through your torso, legs and feet, down into the earth through your bubbling well. The bubbling well, or bubbling spring, is an acupressure point on your feet between your second and third toes, just behind the ball of your foot, about one and half inches from your toes. It is the sensitive soft spot between the ball and the arch of the foot, and is also know as the Kidney 1 point in reflexology and acupuncture. Its official name is yong quan, which translates as "gushing fountainhead" or "surging spring." The kidney meridian is a water meridian, and this point is where it begins. It is considered the one point on the body where your chi connects with and feeds off the chi of the earth. Martial arts practitioners will be familiar with this spot because it is used to center balance. If you are properly centered on your bubbling well, you can not be knocked down by an opponent or even fall off a horse.

To use the bubbling well, imagine your exhalations flowing down through your body, through your bubbling well, deep into the earth, sending used chi into the earth to recharge and connect. When you inhale, bring fresh, empowered earth chi back up into your body through your bubbling spring, up through your veins and organs, into the very center of your being.

# Grounding & Clearing

# With Colors and Chakras

Our human eyes and minds are designed to react to color. Color influences our mood, our appetite, and our health. In nature, they can indicate something that is special to eat, or too dangerous to taste. Colors can relax us, or stimulate us; engage us, or repel us. There are actually entire companies whose primary purpose is to research the effect of colors on our mood, and their findings are used by corporations and marketing advisors to influence what we buy and wear.

There are colors that resonate to the chakras, or different energy centers, in the body, and there are colors that correlate with different issues or dis-eases that need clearing.

You can use color by wearing a particular shade with intention, or painting a room for a particular energetic effect. You may decide to incorporate color when you choose which stone or candle to work with in ritual and meditation. You might only drink and consume certain colors while you are trying to heal, or you may choose certain shades of food to harmonize the energy patterns of your guests.

A wonderful way to use color for healing is to take the time to visualize a color flowing throughout each and every part of your body and then radiating out from your head, feet and body like a star, brighter and brighter, during meditation or before you go to sleep. You can also find sunglasses in almost any shade you would like to work with, or use colored light bulbs in a room while you relax.

In this chapter, we will focus on all the colors of the rainbow plus a few other basic colors: Black, Brown, Red, Orange, Yellow, Green, Pink, Blue, Violet, Indigo, White, Silver and Gold.

*Black*

Black generally represents negative energy, which here does not mean bad energy, but rather a void or lack of energy. Black is used most often to repel psychic attacks and dispel unwanted energy. It is very often used as a protective color that mirrors back energy to where it originated. When you see it in an aura or body, it may represent anger or dis-ease. It is connected with the first chakra, and can be used to conduct unwanted energy to the ground.

*Brown*

Brown is, not surprisingly, the most grounding color we will cover. Brown is the color of earth and the color of roots. It is a color that settles the mind and body and places one deep in first chakra, pulling up energy from the earth.

*Red*

Red is a passionate color, a color of creation and fertility, of blood and renewal. It is the primary color of the first chakra, and relates directly to the sexual and reproductive organs. As such, it connects us with our male and female sides, and helps us learn to integrate energy from both.

## Orange

Orange helps us with self-confidence and nerves, and heals lower digestion and other second chakra issues. It is very clearing for abundance issues and helps us connect to our true, inner strengths. It is also a creative color, helping us manifest our truth.

## Yellow

Yellow is the color of happiness. It will bring light and laughter into a room and into the center of your being. It is connected to the solar plexus, the stomach, and the third chakra. The third chakra connects us to the physical world, and is where we manifest material wealth and abundance.

## Green

Green is the color of life. The plants that heal us are green. The trees which shade us are green. When someone is "green with envy," this indicates a corruption of the normally giving, caring energy of green. Green is selfless and fruitful, and is one of the two colors of the heart chakra. It is the most healing color for physical ailments, nourishing us with the nurturing heart of the Gaia, the Earth Mother. Use it to reenergize the heart chakra as needed.

## Pink

Pink, the second color ruling the heart chakra, is love in its purest form. It is the forgiving, all encompassing love of dogs and babies. It knows no anger, no resentment in its lightest, purest form. It is the creative passion of red tempered with the wise all-knowing, all-loving energy of Source, of God or All That Is. Use pink to clear emotional trauma and grief.

## Blue

Blue is the color of communication and divine protection. The Virgin Mary wears a mantle of blue because she is a Sky Mother, watching over us all. Blue relates to the throat chakra and can be used to increase one's ability to hear and speak great truths. The color of water, blue refreshes the soul and connects us to our emotions. It facilitates clearing of all kinds. Surround yourself with blue when you need reassurance from the divine, or want a safe, peaceful haven from the stresses of the world.

## Violet

Violet is the color associated with the third-eye chakra. It is the color used to increase divination and channeling abilities, along with the colors blue and white. Use purple to further your intuitive powers and see what is hidden. On its own, it is not a grounding color, but it pairs up very nicely with Brown, Navy or Black to encourage psychic abilities without becoming too spacey. It is a very good color to use to help clear headaches and other such indications of psychic or energetic disturbances.

## White

White is the most clearing color there is. The color white relates to your crown chakra and represents the divine life-giving energy that flows through you at all times. It is also the same color as the grounding energy that flows through your feet from Mother Earth, because it *is* the same energy that animates and feeds all life. It flows up through your feet and down through your crown. White encompasses all colors, and all levels of healing.

*Silver*

Silver is the metal of the faeries, and the color of the next dimension. It represents the connection between your greater, higher self, your spirit and your physical body: the silver cord that tethers us safely to this plane of reality. Silver can be used to augment your connection to the higher realms and the unseen beings on this plane, such as fairies, gnomes and devas. It is both grounding and clearing, and when used in its iron form, protective.

*Gold*

Gold is the color of the divine. It is clearing because it *is* clear. It is no mistake that Saints and religious leaders such as Jesus, Mary and Buddha are all depicted with golden halos. Their auras would have included large amounts of gold showing their innate connection to the divine, especially radiating up and around their crowns. Gold is protecting in that it reminds us that we are inviolable. We are divine. Surround yourself with gold if you need reminding that there is no lack of abundance in this life, and in what you can create.

## What Are Chakras?

The word chakra is derived from ancient Sanskrit, and means, simply, a point of energy or power. The earth has chakras, the body has chakras, the universe has chakras. In our bodies, energy flows not just to and from the heart in the form of blood, but through and between our cells, in and around us, on sub-atomic levels. The body has many small power points, from the crown of the head to the palms of the hands and the tips of the toes. The largest chakras are known both by their location and by numbers denoting their order of ascent on the body. The higher upwards you travel, the higher the number of the chakra. For our purposes here, we will be focusing on the eight major chakras, and some healing and clearing mediations you can do for each one.

These meditations can all be combined for a full body clearing. Always begin by closing your eyes, and quieting your mind. Take a few deep breaths. You are ready to begin.

*Clearing the First Chakra (Root Chakra)*

Imagine yourself seated on the ground. Visualize beautiful, vibrant red light pouring into the first chakra at the base of your spine.

Feel any blockages here being infused with red light, and melting away.

Within your root chakra is the center of *The Intent To Live*. This center of intent involves your will to live. It governs your immortality and fuels your ability to ground and collect energy from the Earth.

Your Intent to Live is what keeps you safe, what shields you from disease and physical harm. When it is damaged, your life-force is endangered.

Feel the red light spinning through your chakra center, and strengthening your will to live. Feel it pulsing through your spine, up and out, and radiating out all around you. You are bathed in the power of creation, in the vital energy of life. Breathe in this healing energy for as long as you like.

When you are ready, return.

*Clearing the Second Chakra (Sacral Chakra)*

Seated comfortably, imagine golden orange light infusing the second chakra in your pelvic center.

Feel any blockages in the will center of your pelvis being infused with orange light, and melting away.

Here is your *Intent To Feel.* This center of intent involves the intent to feel with all your senses, to experience your emotions and all aspects of your being: your subconscious and unconscious as well as your ego, your non-physical and dream selves, as well as that which is rooted in the physical. An underdeveloped Intent to Feel means damages your sensitivity, and can be linked with your Intent to Live. The more feeling you are, the better you may perceive imbalances in your non-physical self, and repair the problem before it manifests in the physical.

Feel the orange light spinning through your chakra center, and strengthening your will to Feel.

Let the orange glow emanate from your sacrum out into your aura, filling your entire energy field with the emotional well-being.

When you are ready, return.

*Clearing the Third Chakra (Solar Chakra)*

See sunny yellow light radiating and filling the third chakra located in your solar plexus below your stomach.

Feel any blockages in the will center of your solar plexus being infused with yellow light, and melting away.

Here lies the **Intent to Protect.** This will center involves the ability protect yourself through the creation of boundaries. Barriers are held in the mass consciousness to shield you from negative energy and protect your path to evolution. If this will center is not intact, then your boundaries can not hold, and you are vulnerable to negativity.

Feel the yellow light spinning through your chakra center, out and around you, and strengthening your will to hold boundaries. Let your self be strong, courageous.

There is nothing to fear in this lifetime. Glory in your safety and happiness on Earth, protected by the light of the your planet's protecting angel, the Sun.

When you are ready, return.

*Clearing the Fourth Chakra (Heart Chakra)*

Imagine your heart and lungs filling with a sweet grassy green edged with light pink, illuminating your fourth chakra.

Feel any blockages in the will center of your heart being infused with green and pink light, and melting away.

This is *The Intent to Love*. This center of intent harnesses unconditional love. Unconditional love manifests in the world as a compassionate flow of energy from your heart chakra. When this happens, love and compassion bless all of creation with the love from Spirit, and you are open to receive unconditional love yourself.

Feel the green light spinning through your chakra center, cleansing, and the pink light strengthening your will to love. The lights radiate and glow around you, imagine you are right in the center of a display of beautiful, vibrant, pink and green Northern Lights. Enjoy the beauty and love for as long as you like.

When you are ready, return.

*Clearing the Fifth Chakra (Throat Chakra)*

Visualize clear, blue light infusing the will center of your throat, your fifth chakra, and melting away any blockages.

Here is your **Intent to Create**. The Intent to Create harnesses the flow of energy from Spirit and allows you to manifest your dreams. If your will is not flowing, your ability to dream and create is likewise impaired. The Intent to Create helps you bring your creative desires into physical being.

Feel the blue light spinning through your chakra center, and strengthening your will to Manifest.

See the blue light pulsing through and around you, dissolving any communication or informational related issues. You are a clear channel for creation.

When you are ready, return.


*Clearing the Sixth Chakra (Third-Eye Chakra)*

Imagine a brilliant lavender purple light streaming into your third eye, located about an inch above the bridge of your nose between your eyebrows, into your sixth chakra.

Feel any blockages in the will center of your third eye being infused with violet light, and melting away.

This is your **Intent to See**. When you Intend to See you see the true reality of the universe, and the illusions of mass consciousness fade away. You will see your way clearly, and things will tend to fall into place.

If this center is not intact, you may have difficulty seeing the truth. When you can not see the truth, your path will remain hidden, and evolution will remain difficult.

Feel the lavender light spinning through your chakra center, and strengthening your will to see. Feel yourself opening to new intuition, to receiving clearer communication from your higher self and your guiding angels. Let the light radiate, filling your being, healing blockages to *seeing* on all levels of your being.

When you are ready, return.


*Clearing the Seventh Chakra (Crown Chakra) & Energizing the Body*

Imagine pure, crystalline white light streaming down into the seventh chakra in the crown of your head.

Feel any blockages in the will center of your crown being infused with brilliant white light, and melting away.

Here you find the **Intent to Receive Wisdom and Evolve.** This center of intent allows you to receive wisdom and know what requires understanding in order to evolve and ascend. When this center is impaired, it is more difficult to receive the correct information you need to maintain a high vibration and stay on the path of evolution.

Feel the white light spinning through your chakra center, and strengthening your will to know and ascend. Feel it clearing the energy pathways throughout your body, filling your being with pure, perfectly balanced Chi. Imagine yourself beginning to glow with pure universal Source Energy from within, until your entire body is glowing with a blinding, beautiful, clear energy. Revel in this perfection which you were born with. Familiarize yourself with the sensation of being energized so that you call it into your being at any moment.

When you are ready, return.

*Clearing the Eighth Chakra*
*& Connecting To Your Greater Self*

Imagine yourself in your favorite place in Nature. Feel the beauty and love of your surroundings. Intend to dissolve all energy flows in your chakra system and light body that is not of your own energy signature which you may have taken or accepted from others. Return such energy to whomever it belongs to.

Feel a clearer, cleaner energy flowing into and through your body as you retrieve energy from all others that you may have given energy unto. Feel your energy re-integrating itself within your will centers, and healing any tears or knots you may have had in your light body.

Imagine silver and gold light from your crown chakra radiating up and out, clearing the eighth chakra located six inches to a few feet above your head. See the light dissolving any blockages there, and then see it continuing to travel upwards, illuminating your higher, your greater self. Now you may embrace your greater self, and receive any messages it may have to give you.

Breathe in. Breathe out.

Breathe in. Breathe out.

Breathe in. Breathe out.


When you are ready, return.

# Grounding & Clearing

# With Symbols

Mankind has been working with symbolism for thousands of years. Neolithic humans painted symbols on stones, Sumerians, Egyptians, Celtic Druids, they all created symbols for the sounds of their languages. These days, we use symbols on paper and in art to translate our thoughts and dreams into a communicable reality. Symbols have power, because we have created them. They are alive, just as we are alive. They are extensions of our selves.

Symbols can be drawn on paper, skin or air. They can be imagined in the mind, or whispered on the wind. Symbols can be used to ground and clear in many ways.

You may choose to wear spiral-shaped jewelry, use star decorations on or in your house, draw pyramids the air around your room or over the body, or visualize them in your mind. You may draw certain symbols over your bed when you are staying somewhere new to protect you from foreign energies. You might draw symbols on paper and place them over prayers to reinforce your intentions.

They are wonderful tools for clearing and grounding, because they *set* our intention. I will go over the basic meanings of some symbols here, which you may or may not agree with. Symbols have different meanings for everyone. What symbols do you like? You can draw your own symbols, or redefine old symbols to fit your mindset. Make them yours. Once you own a symbol's meaning, you own its power.

*Stars*

Star-power. It is no wonder that stars in their myriad forms have been used since the time of King David to protect and empower. The sun is a star, and gives us life. It protects us from the cold, black void of space with its benevolent embrace. And when the sun has gone to sleep, trying to catch up with the moon, the rest of the stars stand vigil over us, every night, without fail. King David of the Old

Testament used to place the star on the shields of his warriors to protect them in battle: These days, the star is still found around the necks of David's descendents, as well as on the arms and lapels of policemen, airmen and soldiers.

There are many kinds of stars you can use. Five-pointed stars are connected to the four elements, with the fifth point representing spirit. They invoke the protection of the elements and their guardians. They can be drawn with the fifth point up, to represent energy increasing, or with their point down, to represent energy decreasing.

Six-pointed stars *are* an invocation: "As Above, So Below." They are made by drawing two triangles over each other, one pointed up, and one down. They show the perfect symmetry of Earth with Heavens, of Man and Spirit, Soul and Source Energy. They increase energy and ground it at the same time. They are Yin and Yang.

Seven-pointed stars are connected with the Pleiades, the Muses and the Faeries. Use them to invoke the playful mysteries in your life.

Eight-pointed stars have been used by mariners for years as tattoos and symbols of the sea, as they perfectly represent compass points. They are very, very grounding, and over the years have become powerful protection symbols for those on the sea as well as travelers through life and time.

## Spirals

Spirals represent energy. When they spiral in, energy is decreasing, and when they spiral out, it increases. Some people like to associate clock-wise, or sun-wise, energy with increase, and vice versa, but I think it depends on your perspective. Choose your own definition.

The chakras are often seen as spirals. Many energy healing systems, including Reiki, use spiral symbols to activate the healing energy centers, or chakras, in the palms. Spirals can be drawn over the body to activate or open the chakras during healing sessions, and to set up a pattern of clearing in a room. Move outwards in a spiral to create a spinning vortex of energy to clear and energize a room, or inwards to decrease outside influences and gather your power within.

Spirals are often associated with the Goddess, the Earth Mother, the Creator. This is because spirals harness the creative power of the universe, and specifically, of our galaxy, the Milky Way. Spirals generate power, pure source energy. It is no accident that our DNA forms in a spiral stream, for the power to create, manifest and energize is also contained in our DNA.

## Squares

Squares represent the four pillars of support in a modern house, and the protection of our ancestral lines through our four grandparents. They send protection before us and behind us, on our right and on our left. Squares can be used very effectively to connect us to the four elements and the four directions for grounding and clearing, and help us see problems or obstacles clearly from all sides. As the Chinese say, "A man watching the game sees clearly what the players can not."

## Circles

Circles offer the best form of protection, as they have no vulnerable edges or angles. To clear and protect, imagine yourself in a circle of white or blue light, or place your home under a protective dome of light which nothing may cross.

To ground, circles are also very useful. You can imagine that balls of negative energy are gently pulled off your body and thrown away, or that you are standing on a circle of earthen red or brown light. The earth, of course, is a sphere, and her shape can be a tool for grounding.

## *Pyramids, Triangles & Arrows*

Pyramids, triangles and arrows are all related. They are all directional, pointing up to the heavens or down to the earth, before us or behind us.

Triangles have two-dimensional objects with three sides, and are generally used to help denote holy trinities such as the masculine god trinity of The Father, The Son and The Holy Spirit, or the feminine goddess trinity of The Maiden, The Mother, and the Crone. It may represent father, mother and child, or the Sun, Moon and Earth. The number three is used in magickal rites to increase power and stamina, and drawing a triangle around yourself invokes this "power of three." On paper, if the triangle is pointed up it will increase energy and help connect you to the divine. If it is pointing down, it can help decrease or ground energy. To bring excess energy in the higher chakras down through the chakras to your root, draw a triangle on your body, starting at your left shoulder, connecting to your right shoulder, down to your groin and back. To bring it up, draw the triangle from hip to hip and up to the hollow in your throat just above your clavicle bone.

Pyramids, like triangles, increase and decrease energy. Most examples of pyramids on the earth were constructed to do the former. Whether they have three or four sides, plus their base, they serve the same function. When you are planning on doing psychic or magical work, imagine yourself entering a pyramid of white light. Inside, you are illuminated, safe and protected. Like a circle of white light, this pyramid will shield you, but it will also increase your connection to divine, source energy and your greater self. Place prayers and objects inside or under small crystal pyramids to increase their intention.

The runic symbol of Tyr, the Norse warrior god of protection, is an arrow. Chiron, the centaur king renowned for his wisdom and strength, is always shown with his arrow lifted to the heavens, shooting for the heights in divine knowledge. Use arrows to direct energy to or from yourself. It is not a coincidence that when shamans pull out objects from their patients who have been victims of psychic attacks, the most common objects are arrowheads, along with feathers or string (also part of most arrows). Strong thoughts and words, whether good or bad, are like arrows sent out into the universe, never slowing or stopping, flying forever through the energetic fabric of time.

## Shields & Armor

Shields can take many forms, shapes or sizes. You imagine that you strap on a shield and armor every morning, complete with grounding terminals in your feet and a helmet that receives clear guidance from your greater self: after a few weeks, it will become part of you, part of your astral body. Before you go somewhere to meet new people, or to visit with acquaintances who tend leave you drained and tired, imagine that you put on a cloak, designed to shield you from all negativity and create a psychic shield between you and the world. You may like to imagine that you wear a giant turtle shell, or a bear skin. You may ask a gemstone ring to take on and diffuse any negativity that enters your aura, or to ground excess energy.

There are many symbols out there in the world waiting to be discovered by you. Find them. Create your own symbols. They are all equally good and effective, the key, as always, is your intent.

# Grounding & Clearing

# With Sound and Movement

Every culture of humans on Earth has an oral tradition. We sing, we speak, we run and we dance. Some of this we do for survival, some for entertainment, but all of it has power. In the beginning, the Bible says, there was the word. God does not reveal his true name, just that "I am that I am," because to know his true name would be to have power over him. Words do not just hold meaning, they house *intent.*

Telling stories at the end of the day is something that began in ancient times, when the communal fire was the only light at night, and it continues to this day every time we tell our children a story at bedtime. The rhythm and tempo of our words soothe our hearts and minds, while our vowels tune and re-align every chakra. Stories to entertain, told with the intention of bringing love and joy, strengthen our chi and ground us by stopping the world. Our ego-driven minds and our physical realities come to a standstill when we listen to a story or a song, when we watch a movie or listen to the white noise of a fan.

Repetitive chanting and drumming are very effective grounding techniques that still the mind. Scientific studies have shown that repetitive heartbeat style drumming quickly changes theta brain waves to 7hz, the deepest dream state of the brain, and the same frequency as the theta waves emanating from the earth. This is the secret to why drumming has long been the shaman's most successful tool for entering trance states for healing and grounding work. If you don't want to drum or chant out loud, you can repeat a mantra silently in your head. It can be a simple sound, such as "Ah" or "Om," or an affirmation such as "I am here, I am joy." Play with it. You may change your mantra daily, or you may stick with one for life.

Even singing along with music in the car can still the mind and raise energy in the body. Be mindful of what you sing, and what you speak. Choose songs or sounds with heartfelt words, filled with joy and wonder. While many popular songs are fun to sing along with, many speak of heartache and betrayal: singing these songs with the feelings they evoke, sad with memories or filled with longing, will only help to attract more of the same into your life. Try to focus your voice and your thoughts on happy things when you want to clear away negativity around you.

To add dimension to sound, incorporate movement with your singing or chanting. Use your hands to gather up energy from the sky and the ground. Stamp your feet to stimulate your energy receptors. Close your eyes and see if you sense any energy drains or attachments in your aura. These may look like tubes connected to your body, or dark blobby shadows. Snap your fingers where they connect to your body (the sound helps break the connection) and gently fling the negative energy away from you or shake it off your hands.

Are you tired? Lie on the ground, feeling the earth loving you. Roll around, picking up all the energy that is rising up from the earth. Get up slowly and raise your arms to the sky and feel the energy of the sun and the moon and your higher self streaming down into the palms of your hands and your fingertips, flowing down through your entire body. Sway to and fro, gently realigning your chakras and awakening your kundalini, the serpent fire within you, activating every strand of your DNA. Feel the joy of source fill you. Dance. Love. Laugh. Sing. This is what you are here to do.

Dancing is a wonderfully grounding and energizing activity. Most dancing is a primal, root chakra activity that expands your heart chakra by connecting your feet with your heart. Some dancing, like waltzing and line-dancing, also reach deeply into the second chakra, connecting us to society and mass consciousness. Whether you dance at a nightclub, cotillion, around a blazing fire or in the privacy of your own living room, when you dance you activate your basic connection to the earth and all its creatures. Dancing always activates your joy centers, and when you are joy-full, you are also energy-full.

Through dancing and movement, you can also become your favorite animal or spirit guide. If you desire the protection and caring of mother bear in your life, *become* mother bear through movement. Prowl. Growl. Paw the ground and snuffle. Lumber and roar. Feel Bear energy entering you through your feet, imagine your body becoming denser, larger, furrier.

Or maybe you wish to be free like a gazelle, or fly like an eagle. Let your body move and sway, leap and flap, as you become your animal. Animals are always grounded, always open and clear. It is part of their inherent psyche, that they have chosen not become muddled in the ways that we do. By dancing our animals, we too can experience the grounded freedom they have.

Maybe you are walking to work, and you feel like it would be too silly to dance your way along the streets of your city? That is OK. As you walk, breathe deeply. Imagine that the air you breathe is pure, perfect, clean. As it enters your aura, any pollutants are purified by the white light that surrounds you. Breathe in the air. Every breath fills your body with energy, oxygenates your lungs and emboldens your soul. You are pure light, and every breath you take makes you lighter and lighter. Every time your foot hits the ground, imagine excess energy pulsing off of you, releasing in small atomic bursts. As you raise your foot up, you draw the energy of the earth to you, into you. You are grounding. Secure. Safe and Free. You can use this method anytime you are walking or exercising, whether you are indoors or outdoors.

# GROUNDING & CLEARING

# WITH FOOD AND WATER

There is no food that can feed us which is not of the earth, from the earth. Until we learn to subsist off air, we are definitely earth-based beings. The food chain begins with plants, which consume the energy of the sun (direct source energy) and the energy of the earth (grounded source energy.) Plants are eaten by herbivores and omnivores, who in turn are eaten by carnivores. All, in the end, return their energy to the earth at the end of their life cycles to feed the next cycle.

That said, there is no food on this planet that is not inherently grounding. When we eat, we are serving our most basic instinct: to fuel the body and survive on a physical level. Water also fulfills a basic survival need, fueling us by increasing our energetic conductivity. Absolutely pure water is not a good energy conductor: demineralized water is even used as a coolant in high-powered radio amplifiers. But when you add minute amounts of salt or minerals, which carry earth energy, you create a perfect electric conductor. This is the reason we require salt in our diets. Our tears, our blood, our mucus, they are all salty as a symptom of our aptitude for energy transfer.

Water represents the emotions, our connection to source and our higher self. It is a transport to higher realms and higher energies. Holy, blessed water is used within many religions to heal the sick and cast out demons. It is used to sanctify new life, to bless unions and individuals. Eons of dreams, visions, prophecies have all been delivered at holy wells and springs. When you take water into your body, you feed your soul. Every cell in your body rejoices when you take a drink of water, beaming with renewed life and vigor. In the blood, it combines with our precious salts and minerals to carry the essence of life on its back and electrify our body, our soul's vehicle on this planet.

Choose your water carefully. Always test your well and/or tap water at a new home for impurities, and take steps to ensure your water remains clean. Whenever possible, drink spring water over distilled or chlorinated water. Masaru Emoto, author of "Messages in Water," has found that the crystalline structure of water varies greatly depending on its origins. He found that processed water is energetically "dead", and fails to form the beautiful crystals that natural water will form when frozen. Furthermore, he has found that water that receives positive prayer thoughts or words projected onto it (whether mentally, vocally, or in written form by taping a piece of paper on to a bottle) will form the most beautiful crystals, and water given negative thoughts such as "You Fool" or "Adolph Hitler" will form crystals as damaged looking as polluted waterways. The implication for our drinking water is that if we want our cells to remain healthy, beautiful and perfectly formed, we should also drink water of that quality: our bodies are 80 percent water, and the water we drink on a daily basis is what sustains our body chemistry.

At Fujiwara Dam in Japan, the water is horribly polluted and does not form crystals. After Buddhist prayer for one hour over the water at the dam, the water was able to form a radiant crystal. If you do not have access to good water, pray over it. You don't need to pray over your water for an hour, simply sending it thoughts of love and gratitude will work wonders (these two words were found by Emoto's team to have the most positive benefits on water crystal formation). Or, write positive words like "love" or "joy" on your glass.

Water does not have to be imbibed to clear us. Baptism is an old, well-known use of water to clean the soul, and every bath and shower we take has the ability to wash away negative energy that we may have accumulated over the course of the day. Consecrate your showers, baths and sinks as places of holy cleansing by sprinkling some pure salt over them every few months. Draw symbols over them if you wish, or place crystals around the room. When you take a bath, add some salt to the water for grounding and purification. Essential oils can be used in a similar manner (see the following chapter, Grounding & Clearing with Scent.) Candles in the appropriate color and scent can be burned.

When you visit the ocean, lakes, waterfalls or streams of the land, ask the blessing of the local devas, and then proceed enjoy the healing powers of the waters. If you have your own well or body of water on your property, sit on that spot and ask the devas on your property to bless your home and family, and thank them for the life-giving waters they share with you.

## Foods to Help You Ground & Clear

Although all foods are, on some level, grounding, certain foods are better than others at stimulating the root chakra, while other foods work better on higher chakras. Also, keep in mind that every body is different. Your body may react differently to certain foods than the rest of your friends or family. Pay attention to what works for you. Ask your guides or a pendulum. Keep a food journal. Stay in tune with your body, and it will keep you informed of what it needs. The following paragraphs cover foods that are generally grounding or clearing for most people.

Root vegetables and high-protein foods are very grounding. Potatoes, beets, carrots, turnips, celeriac, eggs, meat, nuts and beans are just a few examples of such foods. These foods seat us firmly in our lower chakras and fuel us with large amounts of grounding earth energy. Dried foods are also very grounding, whether they are meat, vegetable or fruit, due to their archetypal connection to survival in the mass consciousness.

To clear your root and sacral chakras, eat spices like horseradish and hot peppers, garlic and onions. Sunny foods like ginger, turmeric, cumin, and oranges clear the self-loathing and indecision in the solar plexus chakra, while all berries, black pepper, lavender, rosewater and sage clear the heart and throat areas.

On the sweet side, sugar and honey are very grounding and calming, while chocolate literally repels negative energy. Salty foods, and salt itself, encourage our ability to receive energy from the earth and the sun, and let our body's energy centers flow as intended.

Dairy, on the other hand, slows the flow of energy within the body, helping those who have an over-abundance of energy running through them to better utilize the information they are receiving. Dairy can also reduce energy leakage and enhance psychic reception.

# GROUNDING & CLEARING

# WITH SCENT

Our sense of smell is our most basic, primal sense, according to scientists. From an evolutionary standpoint, smell is possibly our most ancient sense. Although our sense of smell is inferior to many animals, we are still able to smell thousands of scents, and research has found that smell is intricately connected to both our ability to remember and to taste.

When we wear or smell our mother's perfume or our father's cologne, many of us feel warm, protected. The smell of a particular meal may bring back sensations of our strongest, happiest times, while certain cleaning supplies have scents that can make us feel lighter, clearer.

Unpleasant smells can warn us of health hazards such as mold, toxic chemical or dead animals. Some psychics report that they smell, rather than feel, energetic disturbances in houses and on people. I have noted that sometimes if a room or a healer is not properly cleared after an intense healing session, a rotten or funky smell may linger, filling the room or following the healer around until he clears himself of the negative energy he picked up from his client. New studies have shown time and again that ordinary household dogs with little training can actually smell and detect breast and lung cancer in patients just by smelling their breath. The biochemical markers that such cancer patients exhale are easily detected by the adept nose of most dogs at the early stages of cancer growth. As if we needed more proof that dogs are man's best friends!

Rich, woody scents are often used for grounding and protection: *Frankincense* and *Myrrh*, the magi's gifts to Jesus, were used respectively to represent the alchemical process of melding male and female energy into divine perfection, represented by Gold. These tree resins are healing to the body, and when burned as incense instantly banish negativity and ground energy in a room. They are still used by both pagan and Christian priests to cleanse rooms before beginning mass or other ceremonies.

*Copal* is considered sacred by most Latin American shamans and curanderas. This local tree resin is wonderful for grounding and clearing spaces, and for invoking protection from deities. *Dragon's Blood*, another tree resin from Asia, is brilliant, deep red, and draws empowering energy through the root chakra to fuel the etheric body and the kundalini.

*Musk* and *patchouli* accentuate the earthy, primal scent of humans, and are very good for grounding and connecting with the root chakra. *Pine*, *Cedar* and *Juniper* all bring very crisp, no-nonsense cleansing to a room, purifying and energizing while they dispel negativity. It is no coincidence that they are used so often in conjunction with modern cleaning supplies.

From the garden, *Coriander*, *Sage*, *Lavender* and *Rosemary* are all wonderful for purifying spaces. *Lavender* will calm the energy in a room while *rosemary* will enliven the mind and spirit; *Coriander* cleanses the chakras, and *sage* invokes strong protection, especially on American soil. *Sweet grass* and *tobacco*, in addition to sage, are both traditional Native American herbs to cleanse the aura and perform blessings. You do not need to smoke or burn the tobacco to use it, merely sprinkle a little on the Earth when asking for her blessing.

There are many options for how to work with scents. Candles can be burned which are already infused with the scent you want. You rub leaves from fresh plants in your hand to release scent, or you can open a can of spices and simply inhale the aroma.

You might choose to burn incense or use an essential oil diffuser. Try filling a spray bottle with water and adding a few drops of your favorite essential oil, spritzing your self or the room whenever needed. You can add small pieces of selenite or kyanite crystals to the bottle to strengthen the spray's clearing effect. For the car, several companies now make wonderful diffusers that work with essential oils and plug right into the cigarette lighter to quickly fill the car with your favorite scent.

# Grounding & Clearing

## with
## Psalms, Chants & Prayers

As we already discussed, all words have power. Words that
have been used over and over again, generation after
generation, by multiple people, have even more power.
Words that have become part of the mass consciousness
exponentially increase their creative power to manifest. For
this reason, I have placed psalms, chants and prayers in
their own chapter. These globalized incantations sometimes
contain more power than affirmations and individual words
with intentions behind them: they are living, breathing
thought-forms that have ever-increasing abilities to clear, to

bless, to protect, to invoke. Every time another person utters their lines, the power of the words grow.

There are many, many of prayers and chants out there, from many religions. You have a practically limitless supply at your fingertips: They can be found in churches, in covens, in books and online. They can be found in the minds and the hymns of our elders.

In the Christian tradition, the Hail Mary is wonderful for invoking healing, blessing and protection and Psalm 23, "The Lord Is My Shepard", is traditionally to clear and protect oneself from negativity. Psalm 67 is used often for exorcisms.

Buddhists use the chant "Om Mani Padme Hum" to invoke Buddha-mind within them. It is pronounced "Ohm Mah-nee Pahd-may Hum" or "Ohm Mah-nee Peh-may Hung" depending on the area one is from. The latter is more common in Tibet. It is said that this mantra carries the frequency of all Buddha's teachings and increases compassion for all living beings (including oneself) within its words. Repeated chanted of this mantra is believed to help purify the body, soul and mind, and lead to transformative evolution.

In Wiccan tradition, no magic or rites are performed until a protective circle has been cast. This is done after calling in the four directions. One walks in a clockwise circle and says this prayer or something similar:

"Here is the boundary of the circle of stones.

Naught but love shall enter in.

Naught but love shall emerge from within.

Charge this with your powers, Old Ones!"

In this circle-casting ritual, the most important words are "Naught but love shall enter in, naught but love shall emerge from within."

Love is all-powerful. Love can cleanse our souls and minds of all ills, and love can protect us from any evil. Buddha and Christ both knew it, and Harry Potter is teaching a whole new generation that true love permeates our very skin to shield us. When we feel love for all things and broadcast nothing but love, love will always find its way back to us.

Even if one is not pagan or Wiccan, circle casting can easily be used to ground and protect. Substitute your own God or Mother Earth for "Old Ones" if you wish.

What is your favorite prayer? Perhaps you have a poem that you feel clears your head, or makes you strong ("Rage, rage against the dying of the light".) Bedtime prayers, like those used to put little ones to sleep, work similarly.

You can always change a few words in a prayer, or leave out a part if you do not feel it resonates with you. Any part of a collective prayer will still tap into the collective strength of its words, and will strengthen whichever words you add to it.

# GROUNDING & CLEARING

# WITH MEDITATION

There have been several meditations covered in this book already, for clearing chakras, working with breath, and grounding with the earth. There is an endless variety of ways in which you can successfully meditate to ground or clear. You can meditate to protect your home; you can meditate to heal your body. You can meditate on the train to work, or you can meditate in your easy chair at home. You can meditate anywhere, anytime.

Many people have the misconception that meditation requires long blocks of time, set aside from the hustle of life, in a quiet, serene setting. Not true! A good meditation can last less than a minute. Longer, thought-clearing meditations are certainly beneficial in learning how to turn off the chatter of the mind, but they are not necessary to the act of meditation. As the Merriam-Webster dictionary says, to meditate is to "engage in contemplation or reflection, or to plan or project in the mind. To *Intend.*"

If your goal is to clear your aura or to ground your energy, and you use your mind to visualize yourself doing so, *you are meditating.* The key to success, as with everything, is intent.

Meditation is the key to centering your self. Before you type a letter or draw a picture, take a moment to close your eyes and take a deep breathe. See the outcome as you desire it. You can spend minutes or seconds envisioning, imagining. Your results will be clearer, come faster, and be more in line with what you desired.

You can do this for anything. If you want to clear your aura, you might imagine your self dancing around you, waving your hands through your own aura and casting off anything dark or heavy. Or you might simply imagine your aura bursting with clear, white or blue light.

For psychic protection, you might want to imagine yourself putting on an impermeable cloak every time you leave the house or answer the phone. When you shower at the end of the day, you might imagine that the water glows and bathes you with universal source energy, pure and white. To renew your soul, you might want to see yourself taking communion, or being baptized again. When you settle onto the couch to watch TV, you might imagine that you are settling into warm sand on the beach, and that mother earth is embracing and energizing you. Grounding you. Or you might see yourself walking through old forest, serene and content.

There is no limit to what or how you can meditate, only your imagination and your will. Remember that you are a clear, perfect representation of Spirit. Whatever you desire, you can create. Whatever you want, Spirit wants. You were sent here to Earth to live, and living *is* creation. Relax, and enjoy. When you feel disconnected, vulnerable, or harried, take a moment to center your self. Close your eyes and reach deep into your body/mind to your still point, where all noise and chatter quiets. Here, you will find your soul, and your soul will find you.

# GROUNDING & CLEARING

## WITH TAROT

Tarot cards have been used for centuries to divine the future and tap into the unconscious mind for guidance. They have evolved into the modern playing card deck used at casinos, and either type of deck can be used in visualizations for grounding.

Visualizing with cards is easy. First choose the card(s) that correspond to that which you wish to clear or ground. You can either sit with the card(s) in meditation or you can simply place the card on top of your dresser or altar where you will see it often. Choose another card that shows how you wish the situation to change and place it next to or on top of the other card(s). It's that simple. In this situation, the action of *intending* change, and using the cards as a tool for that change, is what empowers the soul to create it.

While you sit quietly choosing your cards and putting them in place, the universe is already aligning to meet your expectations. You can also place appropriate crystals around or on top of the cards, or you can choose a candle of a corresponding color and burn it next to the cards, imagining that as it burns down the message is being carried to the heavens. You can burn a candle once, or daily for a set period of time. More information on candles can be found in the next chapter.

## About the Decks

Tarot decks are comprised of four suits, or the minor arcana, and 22 trump cards, or the major arcana. Each suit corresponds with a suit in normal playing cards, as well as with a particular element and all its characteristics. Only one of the trump cards still remains in use in playing decks: The Fool, or Joker. The Fool tells the tale of the holy innocent, naïve and open-hearted, protected from evil by the love of god and the purity of his heart.

*Swords*, or *Spades*, relate to the element of Air, ruling intellect and universal law. *Wands, Spears* or *Staves* have become *Clubs* in the modern playing deck and represent the element of fire. They tell the tale of the fire of creation and new growth. *Cups*, or *Hearts*, are linked to water, the element of emotion and intuition. *Pentacles* or *Coins*, correspond with the suit of *Diamonds* and the element earth. In divination they have to do with material concerns and our earthly abundance. Pentacles and wands are generally used for grounding, while swords are best for clearing.

The Aces in each deck always represent new beginnings blessed by Spirit. Many conventional tarot decks show the aces as the holy grail or chalice, held by the hand of God or blessed by the Holy Spirit. Aces, the Sun, or The Empress are all good cards heralding abundance and new growth, and can be combined with other cards to invite such.

Pages and Knights from the tarot deck have been combined as Jacks in playing decks. Jacks and pages can be used to represent the young, whether male or female, while knights are good to represent men in their twenties. Queens are good for all women over twenty, and Kings for adult men. Is your subject earthy, or emotional? A serious corporate man would be good as a king of swords, while a generous, wealthy woman can be portrayed as the queen of pentacles.

You can use the characteristics of the corresponding element, or you may prefer to match the pictures on the cards to choose your suit, or. Is the person fair or dark? Generally, Dark haired people are represented by pentacles, red heads and lighter brunettes are wands, and swords or cups are used to portray the lighter hair colors.

A move or a trip can be represented by the two of wands, the knight of wands, or the six of swords. A romantic relationship can be the two of cups or the lovers, while a new child can be the empress or the sun. A new project can also be the sun; a great card for partnerships is the three of cups. Business success can be portrayed by the three of wands or the nine of cups, as well as the three, seven or eight of pentacles. General abundance can be portrayed by the nine or ten of pentacles, or the ten of cups.

Illness is generally shown in the four of swords, while heartbreak or betrayal are shown in the three or ten of swords. The nine of swords shows general distress over loved ones.

There are many more cards and meanings in the tarot, and there are many books which go further into tarot and how to use it for divination and creation. *Tarot Spells*, by Janina Renee, is a very good place to begin, with basic layouts for many kinds of manifestation and healing.

# Grounding & Clearing
# with Candles and Fire

Fire consumes. Fire is a living, breathing tool for creation and clearing. Fire ceremonies have been around for almost as long as there have been man-made fires. We can work with fire to enter meditative state, communicate with other dimensions, or to burn away that which burdens and confuses us.

Fire ceremonies are used to create new visions and do away with the old, tired aspects of your past. You can use any form of fire for a fire ceremony. You can use a candle flame, a bon-fire, kindling in a cauldron or logs in a fireplace. You can even use the flames off a gas stove. The only requirement is to have a constant burning flame: the flame from a lighter or a match will generally not burn long enough to complete the entire ceremony.

To begin with, choose a time for your fire ceremony. You can perform them at any time, but many people use astronomical events as their guide. Many native tribes performed fire ceremonies every full moon, when the power and pull of the moon was at its highest. For new beginnings and clearing the past, new moons are best. You may want to choose a day which falls on a certain astrological sign, or using numerology.

Once you are ready, prepare your burn site by clearing away flammable materials. If you are building your fire outside, you can dig a shallow pit in the earth and ring it with stones to help keep the fire contained. As you build your fire, thank your materials for their life on earth, and for their life-giving ability to burn. Call in the directions, the elements, God, the creator, Mother Earth, ancestors, or any other spiritual guides or protectors you work with. Focus on the fire and give thanks for its heat and power. Spend some time using the flicker of flame to focus your intent, your will.

On a piece of paper, write words or draw images to describe the current reality you would like to create. Offer a prayer, and visualize the power of the fire as your protector, your friend. Whatever you give to the flame, the flame will consume, and release in the form of creative energy. If there is an issue you wish to end or something you need help clearing, see that happening as you feed your words and images to the fire. See the fire as a living, breathing being, inhaling your wishes and exhaling your new reality.

Sit for as long as you need to, focusing your intent until you feel your will reached its apex and has been achieved. Of course, you may not have been sitting – it is entirely appropriate to dance around the fire to build energy, to sing or chant, to leap and whirl if you feel moved to do so.

A few words on fire safety: Do not leave an open fire unattended. Never burn pressure treated wood (which releases toxic gasses), colored paper (including magazines, newspaper inserts, and catalogs) or painted wood which will release heavy metals and other chemicals into the air. Only burn brush piles if you are sure there is no poison ivy, poison sumac or poison oak in them, as the smoke can cause serious respiratory discomfort and other problems. When you are finished, make sure that the fire is properly extinguished or that it can burn safely.

## Candles

Candles can be used to perform fire ceremonies with their magical, constant flame. The fact that candles also disappear as they burn is significant. You can "program" or "charge" a candle to perform certain duties as it burns down. You can program it to increase the energy of a prayer as it burns, or to diminish and release negativity as it burns. To charge a candle, hold the candle and both hands and quietly visualize what is it you want the candle to do. If you wish, you can write a prayer or spell that states clearly what the candle is to do, such as:

"On this full moon
let your light shine forth, showing the path
and lighting my way.

As your flame burns,
may all obstacles cease,
minute after minute,
day after day.

Blessed Be. Amen."

You can also anoint the candle before, after, or while you empower it with prayer. Anointing uses oils, often scented with essential oils chosen for their specific metaphysical properties, to bless the candles. Holy or blessed water can also be used. Simply put a few drops on the candle and rub the oil into the candle using directional strokes. If you stroke the candle upwards towards the wick, this is good for increasing power and growth prayers. Downward strokes are helpful with prayers of decrease and removal. Bi-directional strokes are good for awakening and energizing prayers. You can also use a twisting spiral motion to create vortexes of energy.

Once your candle has been prepared, you may light it and perform your fire ceremony. You can let the candle burn down in one setting, or burn it for a prescribed amount of hours every day for a specific amount of time. Chime candles and Sabbath candles come in smaller sizes and generally burn for 1-2 hours. Chime candles come in many colors, and white Sabbath candles can be found in most supermarkets in the Jewish food area. Tea lights also burn for only a couple of hours, while votives last for several. Many markets also carry tall glass candles that burn safely for seven days, generally near the Spanish or Latino food sections, and many new age shops carry candles that are already charged and anointed for specific healing or clearing uses. Wiccan stores also carry candles with seven knobs on them – burn one knob per day for seven-day magic, or program each knob to perform a separate task related to your vision.

Wherever you burn your candle, be sure that it is safe from curious little hands and whiskers, as well as away from curtains and wall hangings. Fire magic is powerful, and must be respected, lest its power consume more than intended.

# Grounding & Clearing

# with Creation

When you create, you are naturally grounding. When you create, you are acting as god, or spirit, intended. You are here, on this planet, to create. Not just to pro-create, to breed, but to create on a daily basis. Every thought you think is an act of creation. Your every wish and desire directly impact your reality.

Therefore, when you sit down and intentionally engage in acts of creative joy, then you are clearing your mind and gathering energy from the universe around you. When you create, your body and mind naturally begin to draw energy from the earth and from Spirit. Your dialogue with your greater self and with source energy flows intuitively. Creation is the best thing you can do to heal your body, mind or soul.

You do not need to be an artist or a writer. You do not need to know how to bake or sew. When you plant a seed or rake your lawn, you are creating your environment. When you paint a room or install a toilet, you are creating your home. When you cook dinner, you are creating your food. You can draw a picture with crayons, glue and glitter for the sheer joy of it, rather than the outcome. You can work on a jigsaw puzzle to create a full picture and clear your mind. You can make a paper airplane or write a letter. You can make up a silly song or hum a new tune, or create some new dance steps while you do your laundry.

ALL acts of creation are equal. All acts of creation of good.

# Are You Really Grounded?

## Take the Test

The following test is not definitive, but it is helpful in determining if you are grounded.

Do you find it hard to pay attention when other people are talking?

Do you feel ruled by your emotions?

Do you get distracted easily?

Do people say you are spacey or have ADD?


Do you think about the past more than the present?


Do you trip often or have many accidental injuries?


Do you find it difficult to wake up in the morning?


Are you prone to road-rage or other disproportionate anger?


Do you stress out easily?


Do you sleep more than 12 hours a day?


Do you avoid decisions or wait for signs to make all your decisions?

Do you feel uncomfortable in your body?


Do you over- or under-eat?


Do you have a hard time following instructions or directions?


Do you forget what people said to you?


Do you find yourself places and wonder how you got there?


Do you have a hard time being on time?


Do you watch more than 2 hours of TV at a time on a daily basis?

Do you astral travel during the day or at inappropriate times?

Do you have a hard time distinguishing your dreams from reality?

## Scoring the Test

All "Yes" answers denote elements of un-grounded thought patterns or behavior. Everybody is a little ungrounded from time to time, it's only natural when so much of our being is rooted in both spirit and on the earthy plane.

If you feel you have too many Yes answers, then it's a good indication that you could use some routine grounding work on a regular basis. The methods in this book are a good place to begin. Find your favorites, or create your own.

*Be Grounded.*

*Be Clear.*

*Go in Joy*

*And Go with Love.*

# About the Author

*Maya Cointreau* is an herbalist, reiki master, shamanic healer, intuitive channel and gardening enthusiast.

Maya has been studying various forms of healing modalities for over 15 years. Herbalism is just one of her passions, and she now co-owns and runs Hygeia, a holistic health and metaphysical center in New Milford, CT offering metaphysical gifts, nutritional supplements and healing therapies. Writing has always been one of Maya's interests and she has worked in the publishing industry for over a decade. She now co-owns a small press (*Momaya*

*Press*) which publishes short stories, and has published both fiction and non-fiction books.

She is vice-president of the Indigenous Peoples Learning Network, producing Earth Lodge® Herbals and Flower Essences.

You can find more about the author online at:

www.earthlodgeherbals.com

www.edenisnow.com

www.hygeiaonline.com

www.momayapress.com